SOCIAL
MEDIA
SENSATIONS

Flickr

Jill C. Wheeler

**Checkerboard
Library**

An Imprint of Abdo Publishing
abdopublishing.com

abdopublishing.com

Published by Abdo Publishing, a division of ABDO, PO Box 398166, Minneapolis, Minnesota 55439. Copyright © 2017 by Abdo Consulting Group, Inc. International copyrights reserved in all countries. No part of this book may be reproduced in any form without written permission from the publisher. Checkerboard Library™ is a trademark and logo of Abdo Publishing.

Printed in the United States of America, North Mankato, Minnesota
062016
092016

Design: Emily Love, Mighty Media, Inc.
Production: Mighty Media, Inc.
Editor: Liz Salzmann
Cover Photos: Shutterstock
Interior Photos: Alamy, p. 15; AP Images, pp. 5, 21; Getty Images, p. 5; iStockphoto, pp. 12, 19; Kelly Doudna, p. 17; Shutterstock, pp. 4, 7, 9, 11, 13, 25, 27, 29; US Forest Service, p. 23

Publishers Cataloging-in-Publication Data
Names: Wheeler, Jill C., author.
Title: Flickr / by Jill C. Wheeler.
Description: Minneapolis, MN : Abdo Publishing, [2017] | Series: Social media
    sensations | Includes index.
Identifiers: LCCN 2016934273 | ISBN 9781680781892 (lib. bdg.) |
    ISBN 9781680775747 (ebook)
Subjects: LCSH: Flickr (Electronic resource)--Juvenile literature. | Photography--
    Digital techniques--Juvenile literature. | Image processing--Digital techniques-
    -Juvenile literature. | Internet industry -United States--Juvenile literature. |
    Online social networks--Juvenile literature.
 Classification: DDC 775--dc23
LC record available at /http://lccn.loc.gov/2016934273

Contents

Flickr

URL: http://www.flickr.com

PURPOSE: Flickr is a photo- and video-hosting website and app.

CURRENT CEO: Marissa Mayer

NUMBER OF USERS:
More than 110 million

* **EARLY 2002**
Flickr's parent company, Ludicorp, is founded

* **FEBRUARY 2004**
Flickr is launched

* **MARCH 2005**
Yahoo buys Ludicorp and Flickr

* **MAY 2015**
Flickr's second redesign is released

Meet the Founders

STEWART BUTTERFIELD grew up in Canada. He went to college there and in England. After graduating, Butterfield moved to Vancouver, Canada. He worked as a computer **programmer** and Web design consultant. Butterfield founded Flickr with Caterina Fake in 2004. He left Flickr in 2008.

CATERINA FAKE grew up in Pennsylvania. She went to college in New York. In 1994, Fake moved to San Francisco, California. There, she was the art director of an **online** magazine. After founding Flickr with Butterfield in 2004, Fake remained with the company until 2008.

Caterina Fake

Stewart Butterfield

CHAPTER 1

What Is Flickr?

Imagine you're at Bryce Canyon National Park in Utah. The view is breathtaking! You take photos of the dusty red rock towers against the blue sky. You want to share those photos with your friends. Maybe you are hoping to be a photographer. So, you want many people to see your work. Flickr can help!

Flickr is a photo-sharing website and app. Each user creates a profile and can then follow and connect with other Flickr users. Flickr users **upload** photos and videos to their Flickr pages. Users can add **captions** and other information about the images. Then the users can organize their photos into digital albums.

Did You Know?

In 2015, Cannon was the camera brand used by most Flickr users. The most-used phone camera was the iPhone.

Flickr lets you share photos of your vacation even before you get home.

Flickr users can choose who sees their photos. Some photos can be seen by anyone who goes to the Flickr website. Other photos can only be seen by the users' friends or family members.

Flickr doesn't just allow users to share photos. The site also helps its users grow as photographers. Many professional photographers use Flickr to share their work.

CHAPTER 2

Love and Business

Stewart Butterfield and Caterina Fake created Flickr. They were both Web design consultants. Butterfield lived in Vancouver, Canada. But he often visited San Francisco, California, where Fake lived.

During a visit in 2000, he and Fake met at a party. The two started dating. They got married in 2001. In 2002, they formed the **technology** company Ludicorp.

Ludicorp's first project was an **online** game called Game Neverending. It let the players interact with each other in a **virtual** world. Players could also create and trade virtual objects.

Another feature of Game Neverending was the ability for its users to post and share photos. This feature was more popular with users than other aspects of the game. So, Butterfield got the idea to create a separate website just for **uploading** and sharing photos.

After marrying, Fake and Butterfield lived in Vancouver, where they started Ludicorp.

In November 2003, the team got to work putting Butterfield's idea into development. They adapted the photo-sharing **software** from Game Neverending for the new site. A few months later, Ludicorp launched Flickr.

CHAPTER 3

A Digital Boom

Ludicorp launched the new site in February 2004. A friend suggested the name Flicker. Butterfield and Fake really liked the idea, but the **domain name** flicker.com was taken. So, they removed the e and called it Flickr.

It was a good time to start a photo-sharing site. At the time of Flickr's launch, digital cameras were growing in popularity. They were also becoming cheaper. More people could afford them.

In addition, more people were getting faster Internet connections. This allowed them to **upload** photos much faster than before. These trends increased interest in sharing digital photos.

Flickr was a brand-new kind of photography website. Most existing photo sites simply sold photo-printing services. Besides providing some printing services, Flickr was also a photo management and sharing tool. Users loved having a better way to view and share photos.

Storage capability also set Flickr apart. The site offered each user 20 **megabytes** of free storage. This was enough for about 25 photos.

Flickr could provide free storage because it made money in other ways. Companies paid Flickr to place ads on the site. Flickr used the money to pay for employees and equipment to keep the site running.

Flickr also earned money from users who chose Flickr Pro accounts. These users paid a monthly fee to not have to see ads on the site. Flickr Pro users also received more storage. They could store up to 1,600 photos each.

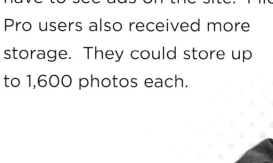

Americans took approximately 105 billion digital photos in 2015.

CHAPTER 4

Selling to Yahoo

Flickr's success did not go unnoticed. **Technology** company Yahoo offered to buy Flickr. In 2005, Butterfield and Fake sold Flickr to Yahoo for $35 million. Yahoo moved the Flickr offices from Vancouver to Yahoo's headquarters in Sunnyvale, California. Fake and Butterfield continued working at Flickr until 2008.

Yahoo headquarters in Sunnyvale. Yahoo later moved the Flickr offices to San Francisco.

After purchasing Flickr, Yahoo made some changes to the site. One was increasing Flickr's storage limits. Users with free accounts got 100 **megabytes**. This was enough space for about 125 photos. Flickr Pro users received unlimited storage.

Another big change came in 2008. That year, Flickr allowed users to **upload** videos. The next year, Flickr released its first app for smartphones. Now users could snap and share images on these devices.

Photo Tagging

One of Flickr's most helpful features is the ability to tag photos. A tag is a label that describes a photo. It could be the date or place the photo was taken. Or a tag could be an object, person, or color in the photo. With tags, people can search for similar images, such as photos of cars or photos taken in New York City.

Flickr users can give each photo up to 75 tags. This allows very specific searches. For example, to find photos of fields of red flowers, search for the tags "field," "red," and "flower."

CHAPTER 5

Growing Pains

After its sale to Yahoo, Flickr continued to do well. However, Flickr faced new issues, including questions about copyrights. A copyright is the legal right to reproduce a creative work, such as a photo, song, or book.

In 2009, a photographer recognized a photo on the car company Toyota's website. It was his photo! He had posted the image on Flickr. But he had not given Toyota **permission** to use the photo on its site. When he complained, Toyota removed the photo. The company also paid him a fee.

The copyright issue prompted Flickr to make some changes. It created better information about how photos on the site can be used. Flickr added tools to help users inform others whether their photos can be used.

The new tools include choosing from nine rights options. These options range from not allowing others to

flickr® from YAHOO!

Home   The Tour   Sign Up   Explore ▾   Upload

LSPhotos' photostream pro

LS Photos

Sets   Galleries   Tags   People   Archives   Favorites   Profile

Demel cafe in Vienna, Austria

Demel cafe in Vienna, Austria

High-resolution image is available at Stock photography by LS Photos at Alamy

High-resolution image is availa photography by LS Photos at

Uploaded on Mar 27, 2010

0 comments

One Flickr rights label is "all rights reserved." No one can use photos with this label without the photographer's permission.

use an image for any purpose, to public domain. Public domain images can be used by anyone for any purpose. Today, every Flickr image is clearly labeled with its rights.

CHAPTER 6

Photo Excellence

Flickr is not the only social media site that allows users to share photos. It faces competition from several popular sites and services. People can also share photos with apps such as Facebook, Snapchat, and Instagram.

However, Flickr has several features that make it a preferred site for photographers. These features include capabilities for searching and organizing photos. Flickr makes keeping track of hundreds or even thousands of photos easier.

Another feature that sets Flickr apart from most competitors is the ability to store and display photos at full **resolution**. In contrast, Facebook only shows about 80 percent of a photo's resolution. Flickr also shows users' photos larger on screen than other photo sites.

Like other photo apps, Flickr offers photo editing tools. It has basic tools such as cropping and rotating. Flickr

Flickr's editing tools allow users to transform photos into greeting cards!

users can also add text and fun elements, such as hats, glasses, and thought bubbles, to their photos.

Flickr's combination of features is hard to beat. Few sites offer as much storage, as smart a search engine, and as fun editing tools. Flickr has it all in one place.

CHAPTER 7

A Lot to Share

Most people like to show their photos to others. But digital photo files are large, so it can be difficult to share them. Many e-mail systems do not allow such large attachments. Flickr makes sharing large photos easy.

Flickr changed how people handle photo collections too. In the past, photos were taken on film. The film was developed into prints. People framed the prints, or put them in photo albums. Then, people would get together to look at the photos. With Flickr, people can view albums by other photographers from around the world **online**.

Building communities and connecting people is another goal of Flickr. Flickr users can follow other Flickr users and see their latest posts. Flickr was one of the first sites to let people post comments on photos. Flickr users can also send each other private messages with FlickrMail, the site's messaging feature.

A family can make a Flickr group for an event. Then everyone can upload their photos from the event to the group's photo pool.

Flickr groups make it even easier to share photos with other Flickr users. Public groups help people with similar interests find each other. Private groups allow family members and friends to share photos just with each other. The collection of photos in a group is called a photo pool.

CHAPTER 8

World Events

Most people use Flickr for personal photo sharing or to build a photo **portfolio**. But Flickr can also be a source of news from around the world. In July 2005, **terrorists** set off explosions in the **subway** system in London, England. Word of the attacks spread rapidly over the Internet, including on Flickr.

At least 300 photos of London after the attacks were posted on Flickr. Some of those photos were viewed thousands of times. It was not the first time Flickr had hosted photos of breaking news.

Flickr users had posted images from a similar attack in 2004. In September of that year, the Australian **embassy** in Indonesia was bombed. And in December 2004, people posted photos from a tsunami in the Indian Ocean.

Photos of these events were also **available** from other sources. However, most of those sources didn't have

The 2004 tsunami was caused by an earthquake in the Indian Ocean near Indonesia. It caused flooding and damage in 14 countries and killed more than 200,000 people.

Flickr's commenting feature. Some people commented on the Flickr photos to express concern about friends in the affected areas. Others commented with kind words for those hurt by the tragedies.

CHAPTER 9

Flickr for Good

People use Flickr for fun, to promote their photography, and to learn about world events. But the site is not just used by individuals. Many businesses and organizations also use the service. They share photos of their products or services to try to attract more customers.

Many nonprofit organizations, such as libraries and museums, use Flickr to stretch their budgets. Many photos on Flickr can be used for free. So, these organizations are able to find photos for their websites, newsletters, and more.

However, companies don't just use Flickr to make a profit. Some use the site to help important causes. One company that did this was the huge corporation General Electric (GE). In 2010, GE partnered with several other companies in an **environmental** project. They created the Tag Your Green campaign.

For each water photo, GE gave 480 gallons of water to the organization charity: water. This organization works to make sure everyone on the planet has clean drinking water.

Tag Your Green is part of GE's Ecomagination program to help the **environment**. The campaign encouraged Flickr users to **upload** photos about the environment. The users were to tag their photos with "wind," "water," or "light." GE made a related contribution for each photo.

CHAPTER 10

New and Improved

Flickr has grown since its early days. Today, companies use the site for social awareness and promotion. Amateur and professional photographers use it to learn and grow in their art. And families and friends around the world use Flickr to share memories and stay in touch.

As Flickr's **online** community has grown, the company has made improvements to better serve its users. The first major change was in 2013. Flickr changed the storage space for all accounts to one **terabyte**. That's enough to store up to 1 million photos!

The second Flickr redesign came in 2015, with the addition of Camera Roll. Camera Roll shows users all of their photos in a **grid**. The photos can be sorted by date. Or users can click "Magic View" and the photos will

Flickr's Magic View can recognize specific animals, such as dogs. It will display all of a user's dog images together.

be sorted by **category**. Flickr uses image-recognition **technology** to determine a photo's category. There are 60 categories, including animals, plants, and food. No one else can see another user's Camera Roll view.

The 2015 redesign also improved Flickr's search engine. It now uses Flicker's image-recognition technology. So, searches don't rely only on tags added by users.

The search engine also has **filters**. These filters include photo size, shape, quality, and color. The filters can be applied to search results without having to do a new search.

Also in 2015, Flickr added Uploadr. This tool sends a user's photos from wherever they are stored to the user's Flickr account. The photos could be on the user's computer, smartphone, or tablet. Photos added with Uploadr are private until the user decides to share them.

These new developments have helped make Flickr a leading photo-sharing website. The photography community will continue to play a role in the future of Flickr. Flickr's users inspire the company to make

Flickr's search engine can find images of the Statue of Liberty even if the photos aren't tagged with those words.

improvements to better serve them. And Flickr inspires its users to be creative and explore the possibilities of photography.

Flickr

A Flickr user must be at least 13 to have an account and **upload** photos. But anyone can search for photos on Flickr without an account. There are millions of public photos that people can view and **download**.

All Flickr users need to have Yahoo e-mail accounts. Part of the Flickr sign-up process is getting a Yahoo e-mail account if the user doesn't already have one. Users can sign up at www.flickr.com.

It's important to be safe when posting photos on Flickr. Users should make sure their public photos don't reveal personal information, such as their addresses or phone numbers. Strangers may contact users through FlickrMail. Users should never agree to meet a stranger in person.

Users should consider the content of their photos. Could a photo be hurtful to someone else? If so, then the user shouldn't post it.

It can be fun to comment on others' photos and videos. But users should be kind. It's important to remember there is a real person behind the camera.

Glossary

available – able to be had or used.

caption – a written explanation of an image, such as a photo.

category – a group of people or things that are similar in some way.

domain name – a name that is the general internet address for a website.

download – to transfer data from a computer network to a single computer or device.

embassy – the residence and offices of an ambassador in a foreign country.

environment – all the surroundings that affect the growth and well-being of a living thing.

filter – a tool that limits the results of a computer search.

grid – a pattern with rows of squares, such as a checkerboard.

megabyte – about one million bytes. A byte is a unit of computer memory.

online – connected to the Internet.

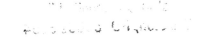

permission – formal consent.

portfolio – a selection of work, especially of drawings, paintings, or photographs.

programmer – a person who writes computer software.

resolution – a measure of the sharpness or quality of an image.

software – the written programs used to operate a computer.

subway – an underground railroad.

technology – the science of how something works.

terabyte – about one trillion bytes. A byte is a unit of computer memory.

terrorist – a person who uses violence to threaten people or governments.

upload – to transfer data from a computer to a larger network.

virtual – existing only on computers or on the Internet.

Websites

To learn more about Social Media Sensations, visit **booklinks.abdopublishing.com**. These links are routinely monitored and updated to provide the most current information available.

Index